T0013251

THE TRUTH ABOUT BUTTERFLIES

Yup.

THE TRUTH ABOUT BUTTERFLIES

Maxwell Eaton III

ROARING BROOK PRESS
NEW YORK

Copyright © 2020 by Maxwell Eaton III
Published by Roaring Brook Press
Roaring Brook Press is a division of Holtzbrinck
Publishing Holdings Limited Partnership
120 Broadway, New York, NY 10271
The art for this book was created using pen and ink with digital coloring.
mackids.com

All rights reserved

Library of Congress Control Number: 2019948798
ISBN: 978-1-250-23253-3

Our books may be purchased in bulk for promotional, educational, or business use. Please contact your local bookseller or the Macmillan Corporate and Premium Sales Department at (800) 221-7945 ext. 5442 or by email at MacmillanSpecialMarkets@macmillan.com.

First edition, 2020
Book design by Jennifer Browne

Printed in China by Shaoguan Fortune Creative Industries Co. Ltd.,
Shaoguan, Guangdong Province

1 3 5 7 9 10 8 6 4 2

These are butterflies.
Butterflies are a type of colorful flying insect.

There are more than 18,000 butterfly species. They live all over the world and come in countless shapes, sizes, and colors.

Mocker swallowtail
(Africa)
One of the smallest
But I have big dreams.
Western pygmy blue
(Western USA to South America)
One of the largest
Orange albatross
(Southeast Asia)
Queen Alexandra's birdwing
(Papua New Guinea)
What do you want?
I'm looking for one of the tastiest.

Butterflies are known for their incredible wings. Along with flying and finding mates, each species uses its wings to avoid being eaten by larger predators like birds, snakes, frogs, toads, and lizards.

Fake antennae may lead predators to attack a less important part of the body.
They're all important in my opinion.
Gray hairstreak
Bright colors serve as a warning.
I'm toxic.
Thanks for the heads-up.
Monarch
Tastier butterflies may just pretend to be toxic.
I'm with her.
Viceroy
SMALLER PREDATORS LIKE SPIDERS, ANTS, WASPS, AND DRAGONFLIES AREN'T AS EASILY FOOLED.
I love butterfly wings. They're so crunchy.

Speaking of look-alikes, butterflies are closely related to moths, but there are some common differences.

THE WINGS OF BOTH BUTTERFLIES AND MOTHS ARE COVERED WITH MILLIONS OF TINY SCALES. THERE MAY BE AS MANY AS 125,000 SCALES IN THE SQUARE BELOW.
Dull colors
Dull? I'm the life of the party!
"Feathered" antennae
Robust body
Poplar hawkmoth (Europe and Asia)
Active at night
Rests with wings folded across back or out to sides
Moth

Most adult butterflies feed on nectar, a sugary liquid made by flowers. The butterfly uses its proboscis [pro-boss-is] like a straw to slurp it up.

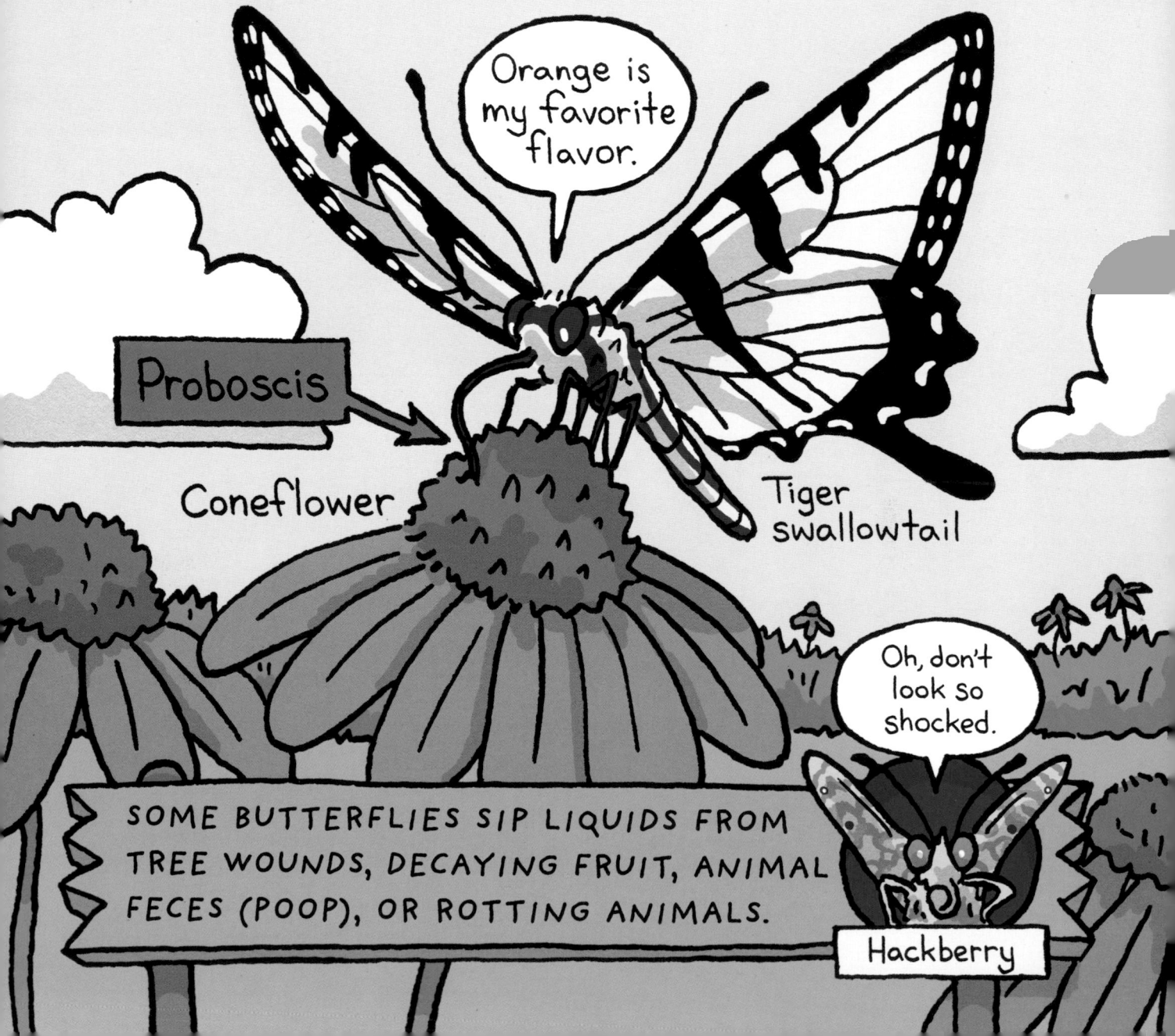

BUTTERFLIES ARE AGILE AND DELICATE BUT THEY DON'T START LIFE THAT WAY. THEY GO THROUGH A PROCESS CALLED METAMORPHOSIS WHERE THEIR BODIES TRANSFORM AS THEY GROW. FOR ALL BUTTERFLIES, IT HAPPENS IN FOUR STAGES. LET'S FOLLOW A MONARCH THROUGH THE STAGES!

Stage 1 The Egg (Ovum)

An adult female butterfly lays a fertilized egg on a plant that its young can eat. This Monarch chooses a milkweed plant.

Different eggs from different species
SOME EGGS ARE LAID ON THEIR OWN, SOME IN GROUPS.
Actual size
Glued to leaf
Did somebody have an egg question?
MOST EGGS HATCH WITHIN FIVE TO TEN DAYS. THEN IT'S ON TO THE NEXT STAGE.

Stage 2 The Caterpillar (Larva)

The egg hatches and out crawls a tiny caterpillar. This monarch caterpillar will spend the next two to three weeks eating milkweed leaves and growing.

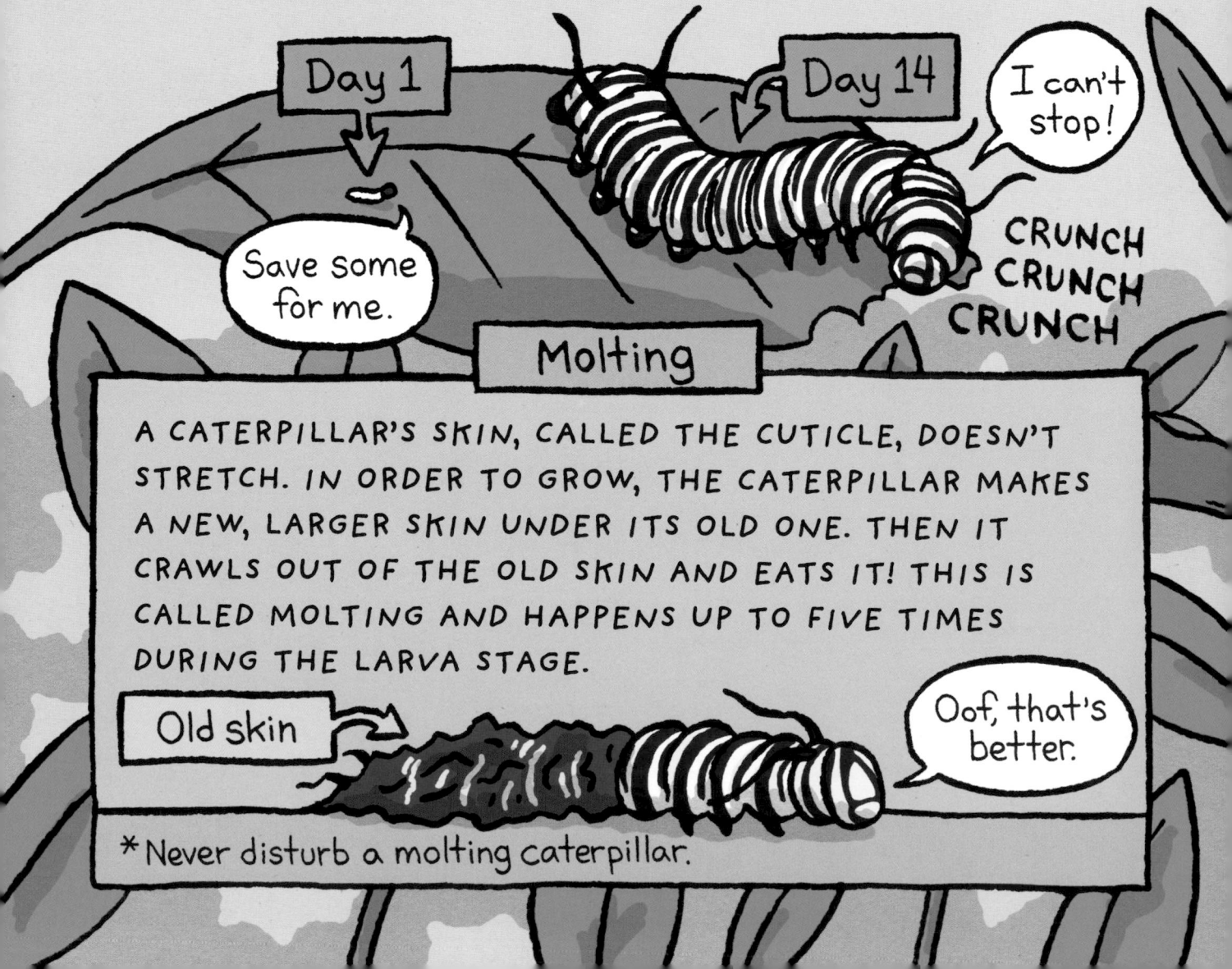

Caterpillars are soft and slow, so, like adult butterflies, they have a few tricks to avoid being eaten.

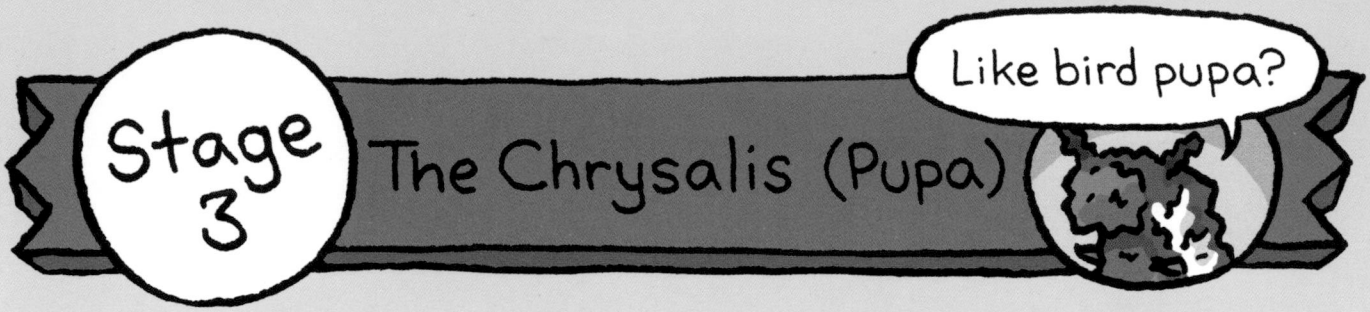

The caterpillar will shed its skin once more, but this time under the cuticle is a hard case called the chrysalis. Here's how the monarch does it:

I weave some silk to hang from while the chrysalis forms under my skin.

Silk

Fourteen hours later the chrysalis is ready and my skin splits open.

When I shed, the couch gets covered with fur.

The incredible chrysalis
Red admiral
Baltimore
Zebra longwing
Clouded sulphur
I wiggle around until the skin falls to the ground.
The chrysalis hardens, and I'm a pupa! Hold my calls.
Ew! Watch it!
Inside, the caterpillar's body liquefies, reorganizes, and grows into the final stage.

The final transformation! After ten to fifteen days inside the chrysalis, the newly formed adult butterfly is ready to emerge. This can take a few hours.

Monarch chrysalis becomes clear the day before emerging.

Chrysalis cracks open and butterfly crawls out.

Hi.

Hangs upside-down and pumps blood into crumpled wings.

Fully expanded wings harden into final shape.
And she is off!
Male
Female
Two spots
No spots
First, some nectar.
I've suddenly got my appetite, too.
THE METAMORPHOSIS IS COMPLETE! NOW IT'S TIME FOR THIS FEMALE TO LAY EGGS.

But before she can lay eggs, our butterfly will need to find a mate. Luckily, male butterflies are on the lookout, as well. They have two strategies for searching.

A few hours after finding each other, the female flies off to lay eggs.

In many places, cold winters can interrupt this cycle. Some butterflies simply die with the freezing weather. Others survive the winter by hibernating like bears.

Monarchs avoid the cold altogether. Like many birds, they migrate and make long journeys south. Monarchs in the northeast of North America fly as far as 2,500 miles to a small area in the mountains of central Mexico.

THEY GROUP TOGETHER OR ROOST ON OYAMEL FIR TREES WHERE THEY DO LITTLE BUT REST UNTIL SPRING WHEN THEY JOURNEY BACK NORTH TO MATE AND LAY EGGS.

Of course, there is one threat that butterflies can't escape no matter how far they fly. Humans are causing a decline in many species and causing others to go extinct.

The good news is you can begin to help by learning more about butterflies, teaching others, and even giving butterflies a place to live.

ANOTHER WAY TO LEARN MORE AND HELP IS TO RAISE WILD BUTTERFLIES FROM EGGS OR CATERPILLARS. HERE ARE THE BASICS OF RAISING MONARCHS FROM CATERPILLARS.

Once a day, remove the leaf with the caterpillar on it. Dump frass and old leaves. Add fresh leaves. Put the caterpillar back and snap on the lid.
I love a clean home.
But remember, never disturb a molting caterpillar!
Collect fresh milkweed leaves as needed.
Snip snip
The caterpillar will form a chrysalis on the lid within two weeks.
Patience, please.
In a week or two the adult butterfly will emerge. Again, do not disturb.
Where's that cat?
Once the butterfly starts to flutter its wings (a few hours after emerging) it's ready to be released.
Safe travels!
I give up.
I knew there was more to life than Tupperware!
Ahem.
WELL DONE! EVERY BUTTERFLY COUNTS.

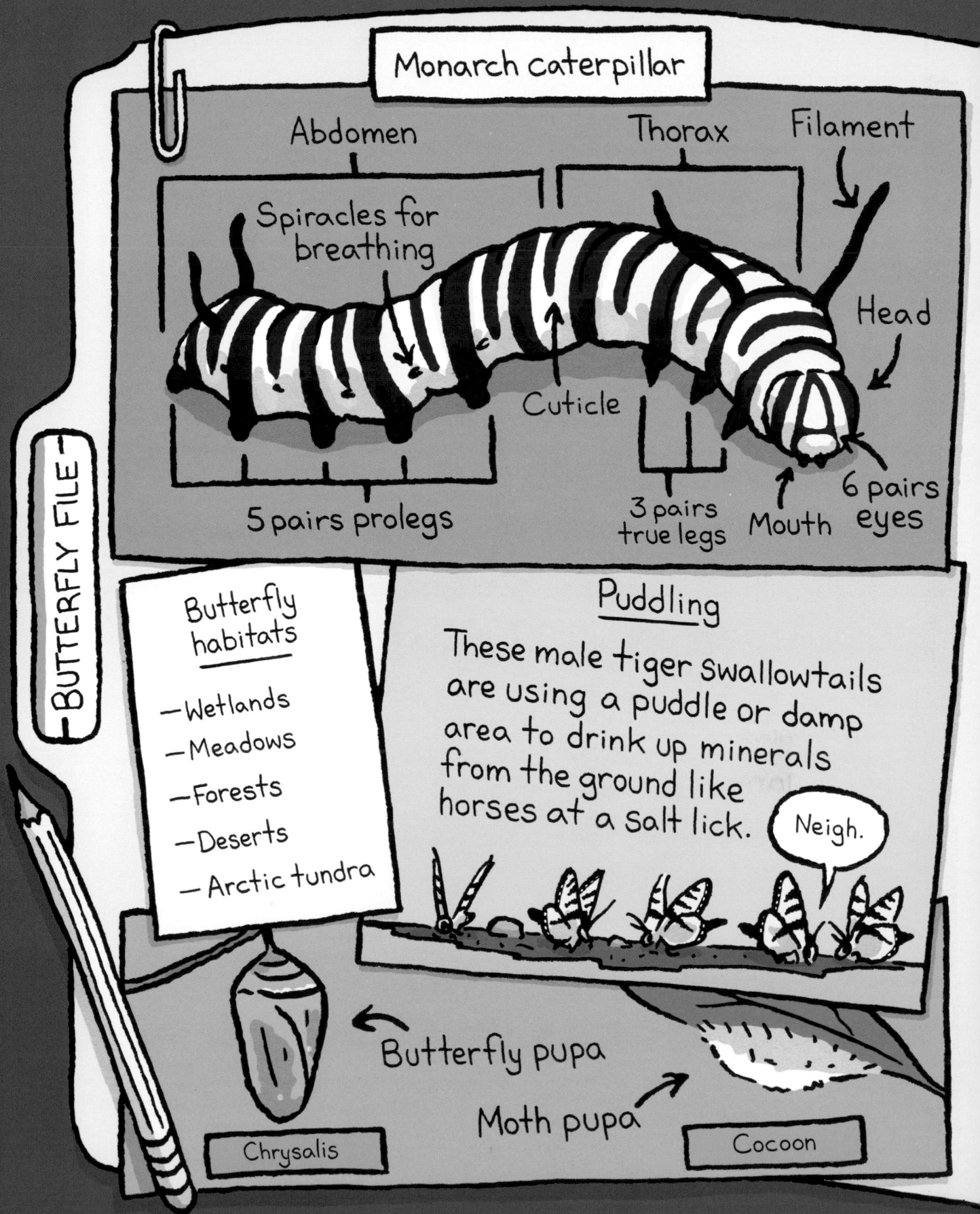
BUTTERFLY FILE
Monarch caterpillar
Abdomen
Thorax
Filament
Spiracles for breathing
Head
Cuticle
5 pairs prolegs
3 pairs true legs
Mouth
6 pairs eyes
Butterfly habitats
—Wetlands
—Meadows
—Forests
—Deserts
—Arctic tundra
Puddling
These male tiger swallowtails are using a puddle or damp area to drink up minerals from the ground like horses at a salt lick.
Neigh.
Butterfly pupa
Moth pupa
Chrysalis
Cocoon

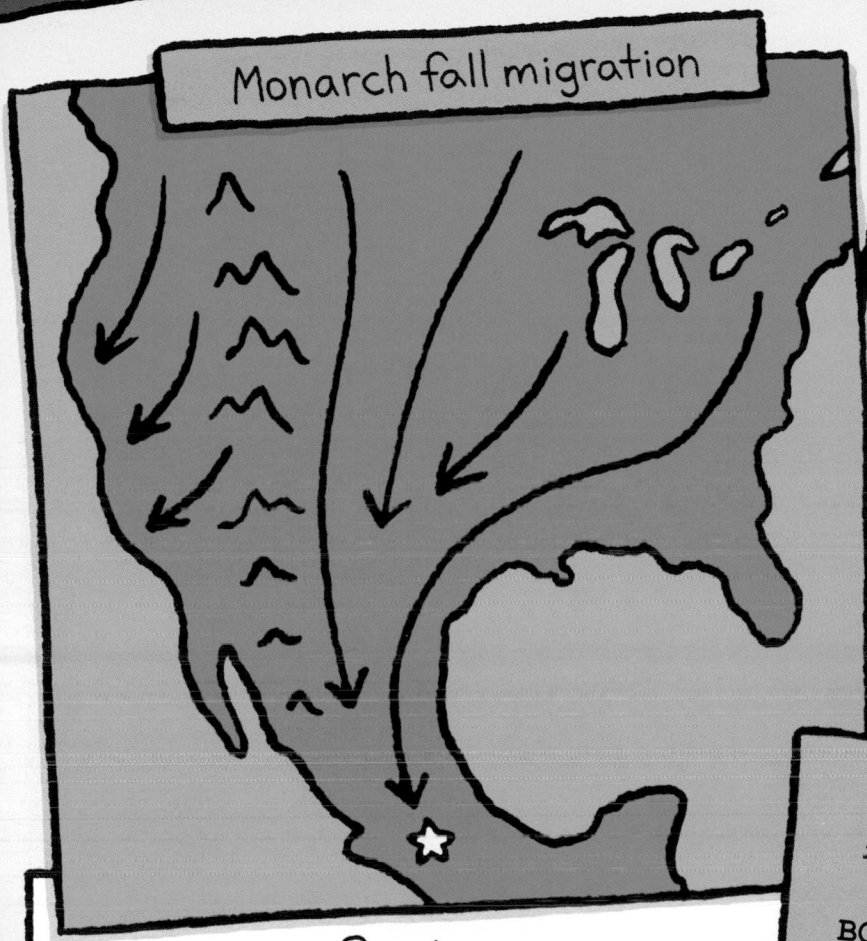

Basking

- Can't move much below 50°F
- Need warmth to fly
- Will perch and use scales on wings to absorb heat from sun

Further Research

BOOKS FOR LARVA

How to Raise Monarch Butterflies, Carol Pasternak, Firefly Books, 2012.

The Life Cycles of Butterflies, Janet Schulman, Judy Burris, and Wayne Richards, Storey Publishing, 2006.

BOOKS FOR ADULTS

Monarchs and Milkweed: A Migrating Butterfly, a Poisonous Plant, and Their Remarkable Story of Coevolution, Anurag Agrawal, Princeton University Press, 2017.

National Audubon Society Field Guide to North American Butterflies, Robert Michael Pyle, Alfred A. Knopf, 1981.

Hello.
Ack!